Ab
Skill Builders
Spanish Level 3
(¡Es lo máximo!)

by Ellen Parrish

Welcome to Rainbow Bridge Publishing's Skill Builders series. Like our Summer Bridge Activities™ collection, the Skill Builders series is designed to make learning both fun and rewarding.

Skill Builders Spanish Level 3 (¡Es lo máximo!) picks up where Español en Casa left off. Beginning language learners join Rosa and Beto to learn more Spanish verbs and get introduced to articles, adjectives, cognates, and interrogatives. New vocabulary revolves around friends, school, shopping, relatives, and emotions. Activities are simple and designed to give plenty of practice and review. This makes language acquisition less intimidating as students learn to talk about basketball, clothes, and popular music on their way to increased proficiency.

Learning is more effective when approached with an element of fun and enthusiasm—just as most children approach life. That's why the Skill Builders combine entertaining and academically sound exercises with eye-catching graphics and fun themes—to make reviewing basic skills at school or home fun and effective, for both you and your budding scholars.

Table of Contents

Table of Contents 2

Continuemos. Primero, la pronunciación
(Let's continue. First, Pronunciation) . . 3

Me gusta la acción (I like action!). 4

Repaso de los verbos AR
(Review of AR Verbs) 5

Repaso de los verbos ER e IR
(Review of ER and IR Verbs) 6

Algunos verbos irregulares
(Some Irregular Verbs) 7–8

Lo que se les dice a los amigos
(What You Say with Friends) 9–10

¡Búsqueda de palabras con amigos!
(Friends Word Search) 11

¿Qué Verbo? (Which Verb?) 12

Rompecabeza: los amigos
(Friends Crossword Puzzle) 13

Repaso de los artículos definidos
e indefinidos (Review of
Definite and Indefinite Articles). . . 14–15

Repaso de los artículos masculinos
y femininos (Reviewing Masculine
and Feminine Articles) 16–17

Práctica con los artículos definidos e
indefinidos (Practice with
Definite and Indefinite Articles). . . 18–21

Adjetivos en oraciones
(Adjectives in Sentences) 22–24

Concepto avanzado: Adjetivos comparativos
(Comparative Adjectives) 25–26

Concepto avanzado: Adjetivos de superioridad
(Superior Adjectives) 27–28

Concepto avanzado: Adjetivos superlativos
(Superlative Adjectives) 29–30

Busca los adjectivos
(Adjectives Word Search) 31

Rompecabeza de los adjetivos
(Adjective Crossword Puzzle) 32

Concepto avanzado:Palabras afirmativas y
negativas (Affirmative and
Negative Words) 33–34

Práctica con palabras afirmativas y negativas
(Practice with Positive and
Negative Words) 35–36

Apareamiento: Palabras afirmativas
y negativas (Match the Positive
and Negative Words) 37

Rompecabeza: Palabras afirmativas
y negativas (Positive and Negative
Words Crossword). 38

¡Vamos de compras! Vocabulario
(Let's go shopping—Vocabulary) . 39–40

Práctica con frases de ir de compras (Practice
with Phrases about Shopping) . . . 41–42

¡Búsqueda de cosas para comprar!
(Things to Buy Word Search) 43

¿Qué palabra es la correcta?
(Which word is correct?) 44

Vocabulario nuevo:Emociones
(New Vocabulary: Emotions) 45–46

Lo que se dice cuando se siente
emociones (What You Say
When You Feel Emotions) 47–48

¿Qué emoción? (Which Emotion?) 49

Rompecabeza: emociones
(Emotions Crossword Puzzle) 50

Concepto avanzado: Los interrogativos
(Interrogatives) 51–52

Práctica con interrogativos
(Practice with Interrogatives) 53

Apareamiento: Los interrogativos
(Match the Question Words) 54

Vocabulario nuevo sobre la escuela
(New Vocabulary about School) . . 55–56

Acciones en la escuela (Actions at School) . 57

Frases escolares (School Phrases) 58

Rompecabeza: palabras escolares
(School Words Crossword Puzzle) . . . 59

¡Búsqueda de cosas de la escuela!
(School Subjects Word Search) 60

Repaso de frases interrogativas
(Review of Interrogative Phrases) 61

Poema escolar aplaudido
(School Clapping Poem) 62

Concepto avanzado: Los cognados y las
palabras similares (Cognates and
Similar Words). 63–64

Práctica con los cognados y las palabras
similares (Practice with Cognates
and Similar Words) 65–66

Vocabulario sobre los parientes
(Vocabulary about the Relatives). . 67–68

Que se les dice a los parientes
(What You Say to Relatives) 69–70

Aparea a los parientes
(Match the Relatives Together) 71

¡Busca a los parientes!
(Relatives Word Search) 72

Páginas de respuestas—Answer Pages. . 73–79

Continuemos. Primero, la pronunciación—
Let's continue. First, Pronunciation

¡Hola, amigos! ¿Listos para aprender más español?

Hi, pals! Ready to learn more Spanish?

Pues, ¡vamos!

Well, let's go!
You probably already recognize a lot of the words Rosa is using. My teacher says that learning takes practice. Let's get started!

¡Sí!

Circle each word Rosa said that you recognize. Then write two of them in the spaces below.

_____   _____

Pronunciation Key

Las vocales—The Vowels   <u>As used in the English word:</u>
A—(ah)   what
E—(eh)   men
I—(ee)   machine
O—(oh)   open
U—(oo)   June

Otras letras especiales—Other Special Letters
ñ—(en-yeh)   <u>Example</u>: mañana—mah-nyah-nah
ll—(eh-yeh)   <u>Example</u>: amarillo—ah-mah-ree-yoh
ch—(che)   <u>Example</u>: chico—chee-coh
rr—(eh-rre: a long trill or rolled *r*)   <u>Example</u>: burro—boo-r-r-r-o

Me gusta la acción—(I like action!)

Color Rosa and Beto.

Me llamo Beto. My name is Beto. Whenever I can, I like to be doing things.

Me llamo Rosa. ¡A mí también! (Me, too.)

Verbs are words that express action. You can't learn Spanish without mastering verbs. Verbs are expressed in a different way in Spanish. Each verb "agrees" with the person, place, thing, or idea that it is working with. To show this, the ending of the main verb changes.

¡No te preocupes! Es fácil. (Don't worry! It's easy.) Here's how it works: In English you would use two words to express the idea "I talk." In Spanish, the way you use the verb tells you who or what is involved.

Hablar (to talk)	
hablo (I talk)	hablamos (we talk)
hablas (you talk)	
habla (he, she, or it talks)	hablan (they talk)

"I speak Spanish" means the same thing as "Hablo español."

Repaso de los verbos *ar*—Reviewing *ar* Verbs

The majority of Spanish verbs end in ar.
Write out the ar verbs' different endings below as
shown in the example:

Llegar (to arrive)			
(I)	llego	llegamos	*(we)*
(you)	llegas		
(he, she, or it)	llega	llegan	*(they)*

Pasar (to pass)			
(I)			*(we)*
(you)			
(he, she, or it)			*(they)*

Bailar (to dance)			
(I)			*(we)*
(you)			
(he, she, or it)			*(they)*

Comprar (to buy)			
(I)			*(we)*
(you)			
(he, she, or it)			*(they)*

Gritar (to shout)			
(I)			*(we)*
(you)			
(he, she, or it)			*(they)*

Prestar (to lend)			
(I)			*(we)*
(you)			
(he, she, or it)			*(they)*

Repaso de los verbos *er* e *ir*—
Reviewing *er* and *ir* Verbs

Write out the verbs' different endings below as shown in the example:

Let's keep working on verbs. All of the verbs below end in *er* or *ir*. For the most part, they follow the same rules as the *ar* verbs, but use the letter e. *ir* verbs take the same endings and follow the same rules as the *er* verbs, except the "we" version. That ending is *imos* as in **decidimos**.

Comer (to eat)			
(I)	como	comemos	*(we)*
(you)	comes		
(he, she, or it)	come	comen	*(they)*

Escribir (to write)			
(I)	escribo	escribimos	*(we)*
(you)	escribes		
(he, she, or it)	escribe	escriben	*(they)*

Cubrir (to cover)			
(I)			*(we)*
(you)			
(he, she, or it)			*(they)*

Depender (to depend)			
(I)			*(we)*
(you)			
(he, she, or it)			*(they)*

Correr (to run)			
(I)			*(we)*
(you)			
(he, she, or it)			*(they)*

Subir (to go up)			
(I)			*(we)*
(you)			
(he, she, or it)			*(they)*

Algunos verbos irregulares—
Some Irregular Verbs

Fill in the tables for these irregular verbs.

The best way to learn irregular verbs is the same way you learn the multiplication tables. You have to memorize them. Let's begin memorizing these verbs by writing them out. You will notice they are similar to regular verbs.

Hacer (to make or do)			
(I)	hago	hacemos	*(we)*
(you)	haces		
(he, she, or it)	hace	hacen	*(they)*

Hacer (to make or do)			
(I)			*(we)*
(you)			
(he, she, or it)			*(they)*

Decir (to say)			
(I)	digo	decimos	*(we)*
(you)	dices		
(he, she, or it)	dice	dicen	*(they)*

Decir (to say)			
(I)			*(we)*
(you)			
(he, she, or it)			*(they)*

Venir (to come)			
(I)	vengo	venimos	*(we)*
(you)	vienes		
(he, she, or it)	viene	vienen	*(they)*

Venir (to come)			
(I)			*(we)*
(you)			
(he, she, or it)			*(they)*

Tener (to have)			
(I)	tengo	tenemos	*(we)*
(you)	tienes		
(he, she, or it)	tiene	tienen	*(they)*

Tener (to have)			
(I)			*(we)*
(you)			
(he, she, or it)			*(they)*

Ir (to go)			
(I)	voy	vamos	*(we)*
(you)	vas		
(he, she, or it)	va	van	*(they)*

Ir (to go)			
(I)			*(we)*
(you)			
(he, she, or it)			*(they)*

Estar (to be)			
(I)	estoy	estamos	*(we)*
(you)	estás		
(he, she, or it)	está	están	*(they)*

Estar (to be)			
(I)			*(we)*
(you)			
(he, she, or it)			*(they)*

Ser (to be)			
(I)	soy	somos	*(we)*
(you)	eres		
(he, she, or it)	es	son	*(they)*

Ser (to be)			
(I)			*(we)*
(you)			
(he, she, or it)			*(they)*

Lo que se les dice a los amigos—
What You Say with Friends

Let's learn some phrases you might say when talking with friends. Practice reading the phrases aloud. Circle the verbs.

¿Qué pasa, Rachell? ¿Qué pasa, Lori?
(What's up Rachell? What's up Lori?)

Nada, ¿Qué pasa contigo?
(Nothing, what's up with you?)

Nada conmigo tampoco.
Me gusta tu camiseta verde, Rachell.
(Nothing with me either. I like your green T-shirt, Rachell.)

Gracias. (Thanks.)

Tengo un disco nuevo. (I have a new CD.)
¿Quieren escucharlo, muchachas?
(Do you want to listen to it, girls?)

¡Claro que sí! (Sure!)

Lo que se les dice a los amigos—
What You Say with Friends

 ¿Qué onda? (What's up?)

 Nada. ¿Qué pasa?
(Nothing. What's happening?)

 ¿Qué onda? (What's up?)

 ¿Quieren jugar básquetbol?
(Want to play basketball?)

 Yo no. (Not me.)

¿Por qué no? Yo sí. (Why not? I do.)

 Yo también. Vamos Grayson.
(Me, too. Let's go, Grayson.)

Bueno, pero después es mi turno escoger el juego.
(Okay, but afterward it's my turn to choose the game.)

¡Búsqueda de palabras con amigos!—
Friends Word Search

Find and circle the Spanish vocabulary words.

Word Bank			
bueno	también	qué pasa	bailar
básquetbol	turno	tampoco	gracias
jugar	juego	claro que sí	muchacha

```
a  p  z  r  s  q  t  n  h  b  m  m  t  q
n  e  i  b  m  a  t  z  q  k  s  u  s  u
j  r  c  j  i  f  i  h  n  y  e  c  x  e
d  a  t  l  u  n  w  c  n  t  t  h  u  p
z  g  m  b  a  e  r  r  a  n  z  a  r  a
i  u  p  g  a  r  g  s  a  r  o  c  f  s
f  j  b  m  p  t  o  o  p  j  g  h  k  a
k  k  z  h  w  q  k  q  h  d  b  a  j  d
x  b  u  o  n  r  u  t  u  u  s  g  y  z
u  a  j  r  s  d  a  v  e  e  j  s  e  k
h  i  w  a  d  q  a  n  f  z  s  l  d  q
s  l  e  f  b  d  o  l  w  v  a  i  y  f
r  a  j  b  a  s  q  u  e  t  b  o  l  m
o  r  d  t  a  m  p  o  c  o  n  r  w  r
```

También y tampoco

¿Sabes? (Do you know?) In Spanish, there are two words that mean "also" and its opposite, "neither." It works like this:

Yo también. = Me, too.   Yo tampoco. = Me, neither.

¿Qué verbo?—Which Verb?

Circle the correct verb in each sentence. Refer to the previous pages if you need to refresh your memory.

1. Las muchachas quieren (brincar beber (bailar)) a sus discos favoritos.
   (The girls want to dance to their favorite CDs.)

2. Ellas van a la casa de Emilee a (comer escuchar subir) música.
   (They go to Emilee's house to listen to the music.)

3. Rachell, Rosa y Emilee pueden (hablar cubrir tener) sobre cantantes por horas y horas.
   (Rachell, Rosa, and Emilee can talk about singers for hours and hours.)

4. Los muchachos prefieren (bailar jugar comer) básquetbol.
   (The guys prefer to play basketball.)

5. Grayson está listo para (pasar escribir jugar) la pelota de básquetbol.
   (Grayson is ready to pass the basketball.)

6. Después del juego, los muchachos tienen sed y quieren algo para (decir beber vivir).
   (After the game, the guys are thirsty and want something to drink.)

Rompecabeza: Los amigos—
Friends Crossword Puzzle

Complete the puzzle using the Spanish words.

Down
1. okay
2. what's up?
5. to dance
7. thank you

Across
3. to listen to CDs
4. to practice
6. the teenaged girls
8. to play basketball

¿Te gustan los rompecabezas?
(Do you like crossword puzzles?)

¡A mí también!
(Me, too!)

Repaso de los artículos definidos e indefinidos—
Review of Definite and Indefinite Articles

¿Recuerdas? (Remember?) Let's review articles. Articles are words like *a* and *the* that work with nouns to give us more information about the noun.

Mira la diferencia. (Look at the difference.)

Do you want to play **a** game?
(¿Quieres jugar **un** juego?)

Pay attention and play **the** game!
(¡Pon atención y juega **el** juego!)

The difference has to do with whether we are talking about a specific game (*definite*) or any game (*indefinite*).

In English, the definite article is the word *the*, whether the noun it introduces is singular or plural. We say:
> **The** ball
> **The** balls

Whether it's one ball or a whole closet full, when you have certain balls in mind you'll use *the*.

In Spanish, the article changes depending on whether the noun is singular or plural. The plural of *a* or *an* is *some*. *Unos* means "some." Decimos:

La pelota de básquetbol   **Una** pelota de básquetbol
Las pelotas de básquetbol   **Unas** pelotas de básquetbol

Repaso de los artículos definidos e indefinidos—
Review of Definite and Indefinite Articles

Write the correct article—*un, unos, el* or *los*—in front of the nouns below.

1. Pasame _____ pelota de básquetbol.
(Pass me the basketball.)

2. Emilee y Rachell quieren escuchar _____ discos.
(Emilee and Rachell want to listen to some CDs.)

3. Nosotros practicamos cómo escribir _____ artículos en español.
(We practice how to write the articles in Spanish.)

4. ¿Necesitas _____ vaso de agua?
(Do you need a glass of water?)

Repaso de los artículos definidos e indefinidos masculinos o femininos—
Masculine or Feminine Definite and Indefinite Articles

Hay más. (There's more.) In Spanish, the articles have four forms, depending on whether the noun is *singular* or *plural*, or *masculine* or *feminine*.

In Spanish, every noun (person, place, thing, or idea) is either *masculine* or *feminine*. And it is usually easy to tell the difference.

You remember how. Many "boy" words end in *o* and "girl" words end in *a*. You can remember the "girl nouns" because a small *a* has a ponytail. And the "boy noun" ends in *o* like an open mouth!

So articles are either "boys" or "girls," *masculine* or *feminine*, and they match up with the nouns they are working with.

The "girl" articles end in *a*. But you probably already knew that.

Decimos:
La muchacha   (the young lady)
Las muchachas   (the young ladies)

Una muchacha   (a young lady)
Unas muchachas (some young ladies)

Repaso de los artículos definidos e indefinidos masculinos o femininos—
Masculine or Feminine Definite and Indefinite Articles

Circle all of the feminine words below as shown. Look for the _a_ ending.

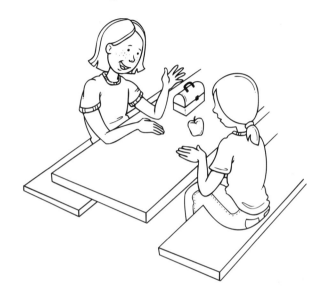

1. La niña nueva de la escuela necesita amigas nuevas.
   (The new girl at school needs some new girlfriends.)

2. Ella no quiere almorzar sola.
   (She doesn't want to eat lunch alone.)

3. Las otras muchachas la invitan a almorzar a la mesa de las niñas.
   (The other young ladies invite her to eat lunch at the girls' table.)

4. Ahora ella sonríe y les dice a ellas: "Ah, sí, gracias. Me llamo Elena."
   (Now she smiles and says to them, "Oh yes, thanks. My name is Elena.")

Práctica con los artículos definidos e indefinidos—
Practice with Definite and Indefinite Articles

Write the correct article in front of the nouns.

El (the) amigo	**Un** (a) amigo
Los (the) amigos	**Unos** (some) amigos
La (the) muchacha	**Una** (a) muchacha
Las (the) muchachas	**Unas** (some) muchachas

1. Beto y George tratan de empezar _____ juego de básquetbol.
   (Beto and George try to start **a** game of basketball.)

2. Tengo _____ película nueva. ¡Es muy interesante!
   (I have **a** new movie. It is very interesting.)

3. _____ muchachas van a _____ casa de Emilee a escuchar _____ discos.
   (**The** young ladies go to Emilee's house to listen to **the** CDs.)

4. ¿Invitamos a _____ muchachos a bailar con nosotras?
   (Should we invite **some** young men to dance with us?)

5. Prefiero _____ muchacho alto.
   (I prefer **a** tall young man.)

Práctica con los artículos definidos e indefinidos—
Practice with Definite and Indefinite Articles

Circle the correct indefinite article according to whether it is singular or plural, masculine, or feminine.

1. Grayson disfruta (un (una) unas unos) buena broma.
(Grayson enjoys a good joke.)

2. (Un Una Unas Unos) juego de básquetbol es casi siempre divertido.
(A game of basketball is almost always fun.)

3. ¿Quieres (un una unas unos) cama para descansar?
(Do you want a bed to rest on?)

4. (Un Una Unas Unos) niñas quiren jugar básquetbol.
(Some girls want to play basketball.)

5. El disco es de (un una unas unos) buen cantante.
(The CD is by a good singer.)

6. Rachell sabe contar (un una unas unos) chistes muy buenos.
(Rachell knows how to tell some good jokes.)

Práctica con los artículos definidos e indefinidos—
Practice with Definite and Indefinite Articles

Circle the correct definite article according to whether it is singular or plural, masculine or feminine as shown.

1. Después del juego (el (os) la las) muchachos están muy cansados.
   (After the game the young men are very tired.)

2. (El Los La Las) computadora tiene (el los la las) espacio y (el los la las) memoría para muchos juegos.
   (The computer has the space and the memory for many games.)

3. (El Los La Las) muchachas van a (el los la las) casa de Emilee.
   (The girls go to Emilee's house.)

4. Por lo general, (el los la las) discos contienen más de una hora de música.
   (Usually, the CDs contain more than an hour of music.)

5. Rosa quiere copiar (el los la las) disco en la computadora de Grayson.
   (Rosa wants to copy the CD in Grayson's computer.)

6. (El Los La Las) muchachos prefieren jugar básquetbol y no escuchar (el los la las) música de Rosa.
   (The boys prefer to play basketball instead of listening to Rosa's music.)

Práctica con los artículos definidos e indefinidos—
Practice with Definite and Indefinite Articles

Write the correct indefinite article in front of the nouns below as shown. Keep the *a* and *o* endings in mind.

1. Emilee quiere comprar _____ camiseta nueva.
(Emilee wants to buy a new T-shirt.)

2. Su mamá dice que ella necesita _____ zapatos más grandes y no _____ camiseta.
(Her mother says that she needs bigger shoes instead of a T-shirt.)

3. Beto no puede encontrar a _____ amigo jugador de básquetbol.
(Beto can't find a friend who plays basketball.)

4. ¿Préstame _____ dólar para _____ refresco?
(Will you lend me a dollar for a soda?)

5. Mejor que tomes _____ vaso de leche.
(It would be better for you to drink a glass of milk.)

6. Bueno. Pero yo quiero _____ galletas con la leche.
(Okay. But I want some cookies with my milk.)

Adjetivos en oraciones—Adjectives in Sentences

Do you remember what **adjectives** do? They modify a noun. We say, "It's a *good* CD." or "I have a *fast* computer." or "That was a *tricky* assignment." Adjectives give us additional information about things.

In Spanish, the simple form is called the **grado positivo**, or "positive grade."

You can expand your Spanish vocabulary by learning how to use adjectives.

Practice writing these Spanish adjectives, which express opposite ideas, on the lines.

grande	chico	rápido	lento
(big)	(little)	(fast)	(slow)
_____	_____	_____	_____
alto	bajo	feo	bonito
(tall)	(short)	(ugly)	(beautiful)
_____	_____	_____	_____
fuerte	débil	bueno	malo
(strong)	(weak)	(good)	(bad)
_____	_____	_____	_____
gordo	flaco	antiguo	nuevo
(fat)	(thin)	(old)	(new)
_____	_____	_____	_____
mucho	poco	pobre	rico
(a lot)	(a little)	(poor)	(rich)
_____	_____	_____	_____

Adjetivos en oraciones—Adjectives in Sentences

In Spanish, descriptive adjectives usually follow the nouns they modify. I would say, "que libro *difícil*," or "what a *difficult* book."

But putting adjectives after the noun is not a strict rule. Sometimes the adjective comes before the noun, depending on what meaning the speaker is after. If the speaker wants to express emotion or change the emphasis of the noun, he may use the adjective first.

¡Tengo un *juego* **nuevo** para mi computadora!
(I have a **new** *game* for my computer!)

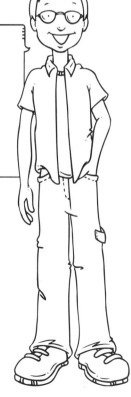

Adjetivos en oraciones—Adjectives in Sentences

Make the following sentences more descriptive by adding adjectives from the Word Bank.

Word Bank				
rande	alto	fuerte	gordo	mucho
hico	bajo	débil	flaco	poco
rá ido	feo	bueno	viejo	pobre
ler o	bonito	malo	nuevo	rico

1. Gra son prefiere comer un sandwich _____ para el almu rzo.
(Grayson prefers to eat a **big** sandwich for lunch.)

2. Emilee tie ne una camiseta _____ y unos zapatos ____s.
(Emilee has a **beautiful** T-shirt and some **ugly** shoes.)

3. Mis padres t enen un coche _____ y también un coche _____.
(My parents have a **new** car and also an **old** car.)

4. "Tiene padres __ _s." "Ah no. Ahora tengo padres _____s, pero un coche _____."
("You have **rich** parents." "Oh, no. Now I have **poor** parents but a **new** car.")

5. George es un muchacho _____, y un jugador de básquetbol _____.
(George is a **strong** young man and a **good** basketball player.)

6. Beto, Grayson y George son _____s amigos.
(Beto, Grayson, and George are **good** friends.)

Adjetivos comparativos—
Comparative Adjectives

When you want to compare two equal things in Spanish, you follow this formula:

The book is as *interesting* as the movie.
El libro es tan *interesante* como la película.

And when you want to express the comparison negatively, you just add "no."

The book is **not** as *interesting* as the movie.
El libro **no** es tan *interesante* como la película.

Adjetivos comparativos—Comparative Adjectives

Complete the comparisons below using adjectives from the Word Bank and *tan … como* or *no tan … como* as shown.

Word Bank

grande	alto	fuerte	gordo	mucho
chico	bajo	débil	flaco	poco
rápido	feo	bueno	viejo	pobre
lento	bonito	malo	nuevo	rico

1. Su colección de discos es <u>tan</u> <u>grande</u> <u>como</u> la mía.
(Your CD collection is **as big as** mine.)

2. Grayson _____ es _____ _____ _____ George.
(Grayson is **not as tall as** George.)

3. Rosa corre _____ _____ _____ su hermano Beto.
(Rosa runs **as fast** as her brother Beto.)

4. Hacer tarea __ es ____ ____ ____ limpiar el dormitorio.
(To do homework is **not as bad as** cleaning your room.)

5. La bolsa rosa es _____ _____ _____ como la azul.
(The pink purse is **as beautiful as** the blue one.)

6. El perrito es _____ _____ _____ el gato.
(The puppy is **as small as** the cat.)

7. ¡Mamá, cuando es pastel, puedo comer un trozo
_____ _____ _____ el del papá!
(Mom, when it's cake, I can eat a piece **as big as** Dad's!)

Adjetivos de superioridad—
Superior Adjectives

In English, when we want to say that one thing is more than another we add *er*. Sometimes the adjectives are irregular, such as *good ... better*, but often they are as simple as:

fast ... faster   sweet ... sweeter
nice ... nicer   slow ... slower

In Spanish we don't change the adjective by adding *er*. We add **más** ("more") to the sentence before the adjective or **que** ("than") after it. Like this:

Basketball is **more** *fun* **than** golf.
El básquetbol es **más** *divertido* **que** el golf.

Adjetivos de superioridad—Superior Adjectives

Complete the comparisons below using adjectives from the Word Bank and *más ... que* as shown.

Word Bank

divertido (fun)

feliz (happy)

delicioso (delicious)

interesante (interesting)

precioso (precious)

difícil (difficult)

amable (friendly)

1. La hamburguesa es <u>más</u> <u>deliciosa</u> <u>que</u> el brocoli.
   (The hamburger is **more delicious than** the broccoli.)

2. Rachell cree que su gato es _____ _____ _____ cualquier perrito.
   (Rachell thinks that her cat is **more precious than** any puppy.)

3. Rosa dice que un perrito es _____ _____ _____ un gato.
   (Rosa says that a puppy is **more fun than** a cat.)

4. La tarea de hoy es _____ _____ _____ la de ayer.
   (Today's homework is **more difficult than** yesterday's.)

5. Sí, pero también es _____ _____ _____ la de ayer.
   (Yes, but it is also **more interesting than** yesterday's.)

6. Jugar en la computadora es _____ _____ _____ mirar televisión.
   (Playing on the computer is **more fun than** watching televion.)

7. Cuando usa la computadora, Grayson es _____ _____ _____ nunca.
   (When he uses the computer, Grayson is **happier than** ever.)

Adjetivos superlativos—
Superlative Adjectives

We've looked at comparing similar things and equivalent things. Now let's learn how to express something that is the *most* or *least*. In English, when we want to say that one thing is more than another, we add *er*. And when it's the most, we often add *est*. Sometimes the adjectives are irregular, such as *good … better … best*, but often they are as simple as:

fast … faster … fastest   *slow … slower … slowest*

In Spanish we don't change the adjective by adding est. We put an article (**el, los, la, las**) in front of **más** ("more") to the sentence, to modify the adjective. Like this:

George is **the tallest** boy.
George es el niño **más alto**.

Remember that in Spanish the adjective doesn't always precede the noun it modifies.

And the article will agree in *number* and *gender* with the noun!

Adjetivos superlativos—Superlative Adjectives

Complete the sentences below using adjectives from the Word Bank and (el, los, la, las) más as shown.

Word Bank

delicioso
(delicious)

divertido
(fun)

importante
(important)

interesante
(interesting)

inocente
(innocent)

tranquilo
(peaceful)

inteligente
(intelligent)

---

1. Mamá es _____ _____ _____ de la familia.
(Mom is **the most important** in the family.)

2. La primavera es ____ ____ ____ de las estaciones.
(Spring is **the most peaceful** of the seasons.)

3. En la escuela, los niños de kindergarten son _____
_____ _____.
(At school, the kindergarten children are **the most innocent**.)

4. Para mí, las bananas son _____ _____ de las frutas.
(To me, bananas are **the most delicious** of the fruit.)

5. Emilee cree que los monos son ____ _____ _____
de todos los animales.
(Emilee thinks that monkeys are **the most funny** of all the
animals.)

6. Y quizas los monos son _____ _____ ____ de
todos los animals también.
(And maybe monkeys are **the most intelligent** of all the
animals, too.)

¡Busca los adjetivos!—Adjectives Word Search

Find and circle the Spanish vocabulary words.

Word Bank

bueno	inocente	delicioso	feliz
bonita	interesante	importante	amable
nuevo	tranquilo	rápido	precioso
	divertido	difícil	

```
l a t d c o m l z v j q i v b l d m
i e t n e c o n i i a q y f w t q h
c m s h d o u i z v n t e q r z t u
i y b i m p o r t a n t e a e q f p
f s o v p r e c i o s o n o y x e a
i l n n d d y i f y l q v p r q l q
d j i a v i o z h j u e n t e z i p
t k t o g v u c i i u w x o t u z x
d z a d j e m s l n g p p g z s b m
o s z i k r t o m f z p t t f c g x
z e k p z t p i n t e r e s a n t e
a r f a j i q w a a m a b l e k w q
q g q r a d d e l i c i o s o z x y
n l h h a o b u e n o y n b x z i j
```

Tan Pronto Como

In Spanish, *tan pronto como* means "as soon as." It works like this:

Vengo *tan pronto como* puedo. = I'm coming **as soon as** I can.

Rompecabeza: Palabras descriptivas—
Descriptive Words Crossword

Use Spanish words to complete the crossword.

Down
1. good
2. short
3. fat
4. slow
5. bad
7. weak
8. strong
10. pretty
11. a lot
15. tall
16. poor
17. little

Across
3. big
6. new
8. thin
9. ugly
12. rich
13. old
14. fast
16. a little

¡Yo quiero un helado grande, por favor!

(I want a big ice cream cone, please.)

Sí, después que termines un deber.

(Sure, after you finish a chore.)

Palabras afirmativas y negativas—
Affirmative and Negative Words

Now let's learn about affirmative and negative words in Spanish. They are pretty easy to learn and remember. Plus, they come in handy.

Palabras Afirmativas		Palabras Negativas	
algo	something	nada	nothing
alguien	someone	nadie	no one
algún alguno/a/os/as	some, any	ningún ninguno/a/os/as	none, not any
siempre	always	nunca, jamás	never
a veces	sometimes		
alguna vez	sometime		
algún día	someday		
también	also	tampoco	not either, neither
todavía	still	todavía no	not yet
o .... o	either .... or	ni .... ni	neither .... nor
de algún modo	somehow	de ningún modo	by no means
de alguna manera	some way	de ninguna manera	no way

En el traspatio—In the Backyard

Notice how **algún** and **ningún** have several different endings. That's because they must match the gender and number of the nouns they are working with.

It works like this:

1. ¿Hay *algún libro* sobre básquetbol en la biblioteca?
   Are there **any** books about basketball in the library.

2. No puedo encontrar *ningún libro* sobre deportes en esta biblioteca.
   I can**not** find any book about sports in this library.

The second sentence shows a big difference between Spanish and English. In English, we add *no* or *not* to a sentence to express a negative. But in Spanish the whole word is negative. The rules are different, but the idea is the same.

See the difference? And you can use double negatives, and the sentence remains a negative sentence.

Language has patterns.
And your brain soon learns to recognize those patterns.

I see two patterns here. First, most of the negative words begin with *N,* and most of the affirmative words begin with *A.*

Second, the opposites sort of match up.

Práctica con palabras afirmativas y negativas—
Practice with Positive and Negative Words

Complete the sentences below, using affirmative and negative words from the Word Bank. Say the Spanish sentences aloud.

Word Bank

algo (something)
nada (nothing)

siempre (always)
nunca (never)
a veces (sometimes)

también (also)
tampoco (neither, either)

1. ¿Hay <u>algo</u> interesante en tu libro?
   (Is there **something** interesting in your book?)

2. No, _____ especial, pero esta autora es mi favorita.
   (No, **nothing** special, but this author is my favorite.)

3. ¡Ah, y la mía _____! ¿Dónde encontraste el libro?
   (Oh, she's mine, **too (also)**! Where did you find the book?)

4. Allí, en el tercer estante. Sus libros _____ cuentan buenas aventuras .
   (Over there, on the third shelf. Her books **always** tell of good adventures.)

5. Y _____ muchas escenas de amor!
   (And **never** many love scenes!)

6. No me gusta leer libros románticos _____.
   (I don't like to read romantic books **either**.)

7. Pero ___ _____ hay que leer libros románticos
   (But **sometimes** you have to read romantic books.)

Práctica con palabras afirmativas y negativas—
Practice with Positive and Negative Words

8. Necesito buscar _____ libros sobre los volcanes para mi tarea.

(I need to look for **some** books about volcanoes for my homework.)

9. Yo _____. Pero no hay _____ libro sobre ciencias en esta sección de la biblioteca.

(Me **too**. But there are **not any** books about science in this section of the library.)

10. Pues, _____ vamos a otro nivel _____ cambiamos a un proyecto diferente para tarea de ciencias.

(Well, **either** we go to another level **or** we change to a different science project.)

11. ¡_____! Yo ya tengo un dibujo bueno de un volcán que quiero usar.

(**No way**! I already have a good drawing of a volcano that I want to use.)

12. ¿De veras? Yo no tengo _____ un dibujo _____ una idea para otro proyecto.

(Really? I have **neither** a drawing **nor** an idea for another project.)

13. _____, tenemos que encontrar a _____ que nos ayude a buscar la sección de ciencias.

(**Somehow**, we must find **someone** to help us look for the science section.)

Aparear: palabras afirmativas y negativas—
Match the Affirmative and Negative Words

Draw a line between the affirmative and negative words that express opposite ideas.

también also	**siempre** always
ninguno none	**ni … ni** neither … nor
nunca never	**tampoco** neither
o … o either … or	**alguno** some
nadie no one	**nada** nothing
de ninguna manera no way	**alguien** someone
algo something	**de alguna manera** somehow

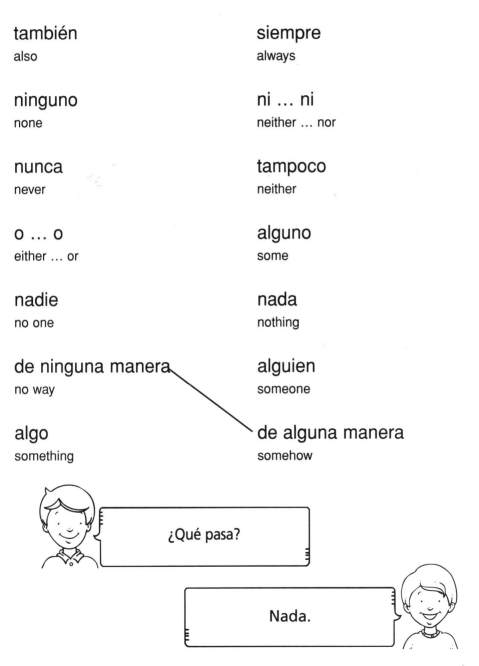

¿Qué pasa?

Nada.

Rompecabeza: palabras afirmativas y negativas—Positive and Negative Words Crossword

Complete the puzzle using the Spanish words.

Down
2. someone
4. no one
6. sometimes
7. never

Across
1. nothing
3. something
5. also
8. always
9. none
10. neither

¿Tienes hambre?
(Are you hungry?)

¡Siempre! (Always!)

¡Vamos de compras! Vocabulario—
Let's go shopping! Vocabulary

Practice writing the shopping vocabulary words on the lines provided.

<u>Verbos</u>   <u>Verbs</u>

pagar   (to pay)   _____

comprar   (to buy)   _____

vender   (to sell)   _____

buscar   (to look for)   _____

pedir ayuda (to ask for help) _____

llevar   (to carry)   _____

mirar   (to look at)   _____

<u>Adjetivos</u>   <u>Adjectives</u>

caro   (expensive)   _____

barato   (cheap)   _____

nuevo   (new)   _____

Necesito zapatos nuevos y baratos.
(I need some new cheap shoes.)

$3.00
Bargain!

¡Vamos de compras! Vocabulario—
Let's go shopping! Vocabulary

Nombres	**Nouns**	
tienda	(store)	_____
oferta	(sale)	_____
talla	(size)	_____
precio	(price)	_____
tarjeta de crédito	(credit card)	_____
cheque	(check)	_____
dinero	(money)	_____
cambio	(change)	_____
bolsa	(purse)	_____
vendedor(a)	(salesperson)	_____
ropa	(clothing)	_____
zapatos	(shoes)	_____
comida	(food)	_____
vestidor	(dressing room)	_____

Tengo dinero para ir de compras.
(I have money to go shopping.)

Práctica con frases de ir de compras—
Practice with Phrases about Shopping

Write the correct verb in the space provided. Then say the sentences aloud.

Word Bank

pedir ayuda

comprar

vender

buscar

llevar

pagar

mirar

---

1. Rosa le va a _llevar_ las bolsas a su abuela.
(Rosa is going **to carry** the bags for her grandma.)

2. Papá dice que debo _____ _____ si no puedo encontrar algo.
(Dad says that I ought **to ask for help** if I can't find something.)

3. Quiero _____ algo barato porque tengo sólo cinco dólares.
(I want **to look for** something cheap because I have only five dollars.)

4. Vamos a _____ los discos nuevos.
(We are going **to look at** the new CDs.)

5. Mamá prefiere _____ con su tarjeta de crédito.
(Mom prefers **to pay** with her credit card.)

6. Vamos a la otra tienda, donde van a _____ los discos por menos dinero.
(Let's go to the other store, where they're going **to sell** the CDs for less money.)

7. ¿Vas a _____ algo para mi cumpleaños?
(Are you going **to buy** something for my birthday?)

Práctica con frases de ir de compras—
Practice with Phrases about Shopping

Write the correct noun in the space provided. Then say the sentences aloud.

Word Bank

tienda (store)	tarjeta de crédito (credit card)	cambio (change)	ropa (clothing)
oferta (sale)	cheque (check)	bolsa (purse)	zapatos (shoes)
precio (price)	dinero (money)	vendedor(a) (salesperson)	vestidor (dressing room)

1. Vamos a esta _____ porque hay una _____ en _____ escolar.
   (Let's go to this **store** because there's a **sale** on school **clothing**.)

2. ¿Tienes suficiente _____ para todo? ¡Mira los _____s!
   (Do you have enough **money** for everything? Look at the **prices**!)

3. Sí, claro. Puedo pagar con _____ o _____.
   (Yes, of course. I can pay with **check** or **credit card**.)

4. Buscamos a la _____ porque los _____ no tiene _____.
   (Let's look for the **salesperson** because the **shoes** don't have a **price**.)

5. Perdón, ¿Puede abrirnos el _____?
   (Excuse me. Could you open the **dressing room** for us?)

6. Creo que tengo algo de _____ en la _____.
   (I believe that I have a little **change** in my **purse**.)

¡Búsqueda de cosas para comprar!— Things to Buy Word Search

Find and circle the Spanish vocabulary words.

Word Bank

comprar	caro	vendedor	cheque
pagar	tienda	dinero	cambio
barato	precio	oferta	bolsa

```
        f  c  c  h  e  q  u  e  w  q
        a  q  c  c  i  b  s  c  t  m
  l  r  q  w  m  q  r  g  j  x  i  c  w  y
  o  n  p  q  r  d  y  l  f  w  e  w  j  p
  p  t  z  j  w  u        c  f  n  r  p  g
  r  c  m  g  p  j        k  z  d  v  l  d
  e  x  v  r              a  o  u  p
  c  a  e  l              c  i  n  a
  i  o  n  z              f  b  d  g
  o  t  d  o              l  m  t  a
  q  a  e  r              l  a  w  r
  e  r  d  e              j  c  k  c
  g  a  o  n  h  s     q  c  y  h  y  e
  w  b  r  i  s  n        o  n  e  d  q  f
  r  z  u  d  n  n  q  o  f  e  r  t  a  f
  u  n  c  o  m  p  r  a  r  b  o  l  s  a
        c  h  j  r  l  r  p  b  t  c
        i  n  b  h  i  c  i  r  s  r
```

¡Mira mis zapatos nuevos! (Look at my new shoes!)

¿Qué palabra es la correcta?—
Which word is correct?

Circle the correct word in each sentence as shown. Then say the sentence aloud.

1. Vamos de compras. Necesito (dinero   precio   (zapatos)) nuevos.
   (Let's go shopping. I need some new **shoes**.)

2. Emilee y Rosa van a (pagar   buscar   mirar) una oferta en ropa.
   (Emilee and Rosa are going **to look for** a sale on clothes.)

3. ¡Qué (baratos   caros   nuevos) son los precios en esta tienda!
   (How **cheap** the prices are in this store!)

4. George no tiene (oferta   cheque   cambio) para comprar el dulce.
   (George doesn't have **change** to buy the candy.)

5. Mi (tocador   tienda   vendedor) favorita está en esta calle.
   (Mi favorite **store** is on that street.)

6. Mamá paga todo con (cheque   dinero   bolsa).
   (Mom pays for everything with a **check**.)

7. ¿Qué (caro   talla   oferta) de ropa tiene Rosa?
   (What **size** of clothes does Rosa have?)

Vocabulario nuevo: Emociones—
New Vocabulary: Emotions

Here are some Spanish words that express emotions.

Practice writing the vocabulary words for emotions on the lines provided. Then say the words aloud.

1. feliz (happy) _____

2. triste (sad) _____

3. cansado (tired) _____

4. tímido (timid) _____

5. tranquillo (calm) _____

6. amable (friendly) _____

7. enojado (angry) _____

8. celoso (jealous) _____

9. simpático (charming) _____

10. antipático (disagreeable) _____

11. sorpendido (surprised) _____

Vocabulario nuevo: Emociones—Emotions

12. deprimido (depressed) _____

13. emocionado (excited) _____

14. contento (glad/satisfied) _____

15. nervioso (nervous) _____

16. enfermo (sick) _____

17. de buen humor (in a good mood)_____

18. de mal humor (in a bad mood) _____

19. preocupado (worried) _____

20. desilusionado (disappointed) _____

21. aburrido (bored) _____

22. encantado (delighted) _____

Lo que se dice cuando se siente emociones
—What You Say When You Feel Emotions

Use **estar + the emotion** to talk about feelings.

	Estar (to be)		
(I am)	Estoy	estamos	*(we are)*
(you are)	estás		
(he, she, or it is)	está	están	*(they are)*

Like this:

¿Comó **estás**?	**Estoy cansado.**	Mi Mamá **está de mal humor**.
How **are you**?	I am **tired**.	My mom **is in a bad mood**.

Practice your Spanish by saying the words aloud as you complete each sentence with the correct vocabulary word.

Word Bank

encantado	preocupado	sorpendido
alegre	nervioso	contento

---

1. Rosa **está** _____ porque su poema ganó un premio.
   (Rosa **is surprised** because her poem won a prize.)

2. Sus amigos están muy _____ por ella.
   (Her friends **are** very **happy** for her.)

3. Ella está _____ con su poema.
   (She **is content** with her poem.)

4. ¿Rosa **está** _____ de hablar con el juez del concurso de poesía?
   (**Is** she **nervous** about talking with the judge of the poetry competition?)

5. No, Rosa no **está** _____ por nada.
   (No, Rosa **is** not **worried** about anything.)

6. Creo que ella **está** _____ con su premio.
   (I believe that she **is delighted** with her prize.)

Lo que se dice cuando se siente emociones
—What You Say When You Feel Emotions

Many of these words are cognates. A **cognate** is a word that is similar in both languages, for example **nervous** and **nervioso**.

These cognates are words that came from the same Latin roots.

Word Bank

tranquilo
celoso

cansado
deprimido
aburrido

de buen humor
feliz

7. ¿Por qué no sonríes, María? ¿**Estás** _____?
(How come you're not smiling, Maria? **Are you depressed?**)

8. No, en realidad **estoy** un poco _____ y un poco
_____.
(No, in reality **I am** a little **tired** and a little **bored.**)

9. ¿Si vamos a la biblioteca, vas a **estar** _____?
(If we go to the libarary, are you going **to be in a good mood.**)

10. ¡Ah sí! En el silencio de la biblioteca **estoy** _____.
(Oh yes! In the silence of the library **I am calm.**)

11. Bueno. Si tú **estás** _____, yo **estoy** _____.
(Good. If **you're happy, I'm happy**.)

12. Emilee **está** _____ porque ella no puede ir a la biblioteca.
(Emilee **is jealous** because she can't go to the library.)

Ponerlos juntos: ¿Cuál emoción?—
Which Emotion?

Draw a line between the Spanish vocabulary words and English words as shown.

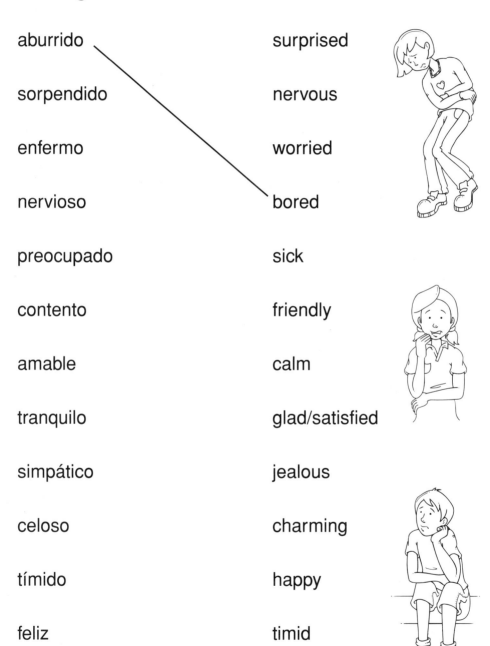

aburrido	surprised
sorpendido	nervous
enfermo	worried
nervioso	bored
preocupado	sick
contento	friendly
amable	calm
tranquilo	glad/satisfied
simpático	jealous
celoso	charming
tímido	happy
feliz	timid

Rompecabeza—Emotions Crossword Puzzle

Complete the puzzle using Spanish words.

Across	Down
2. delighted	**1.** disappointed
5. angry	**3.** in a bad mood
7. sad	**4.** excited
8. depressed	**6.** disagreeable
9. in a good mood	
10. tired	

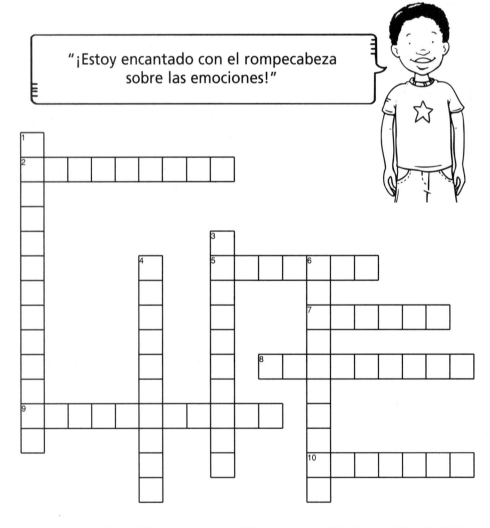

"¡Estoy encantado con el rompecabeza sobre las emociones!"

Los interrogativos—
Interrogatives

Interrogative words are also called **question words** in English.

In English, the main question words are **who, what, when, where, why,** and **how**.

In Spanish, they are **cómo, cuál, cuándo, cuánto, dónde, qué,** and **quién**.

Notice that all the Spanish interrogative words use an accent mark. The accent mark is part of the spelling. It means the word is part of a question.

Write out the Spanish word on the lines provided. Don't forget the accent and punctuation marks.

¿quién?   (who?)   _____

¿qué?   (what?)   _____

¿cuándo?   (when?)   _____

¿dónde?   (where?)   _____

¿por qué?   (why?)   _____

¿cómo?   (how?)   _____

Los interrogativos—
Interrogatives

The same words can be used as **non-question** words, and then no accent is used.

For example, you might say, "My bedroom is **where** I sleep." In Spanish, it would read, "Mi dormitorio es **donde** yo duermo."

Here are a few more question words that are commonly used in Spanish.

Write out the Spanish word in the lines provided. Don't forget the accent and punctuation marks.

¿cuánto?   (how much?)   _____

¿cuántos?   (how many?)   _____

¿adónde?   (to where?)   _____

¿cuál?   (which?)   _____

Práctica con interrogativos—
Practice with Interrogatives

Circle the correct question word in the sentences below.

Word Bank

¿quién?	¿cuándo?	¿por qué?
(who?)	(when?)	(why?)
¿qué?	¿dónde?	¿cómo?
(what?)	(where?)	(how?)

1. (¿Por qué   Quién   Qué) quiere ir a tomar helado?
   (Who wants to go for ice cream?)

2. (¿Dónde   Cuándo   Qué) vamos?
   (When are we leaving?)

3. (¿Cómo   Dónde   Cuándo) regresamos?
   (When are we coming back?)

4. (¿Dónde   Cómo   Quién) se vende el helado por poco dinero?
   (Where do they sell ice cream for very little money?)

5. (¿Quién   Por qué   Cómo) preguntas? Mi mamá va a comprarlos.
   (Why do you ask? My mom is going to buy them.)

6. (¿Dónde   Cómo   Qué) persuadiste a tu mamá?
   (How did you persuade your mom?)

Aparear: Los interrogativos—
Match the Question Words

Draw a line between the Spanish question words and their English equivalents.

who?	¿qué?
what?	¿cuándo?
when?	¿quién?
where?	¿por qué?
why?	¿cómo?
how?	¿dónde?
how much?	¿adónde?
to where?	¿cuál?
which?	¿cuánto?

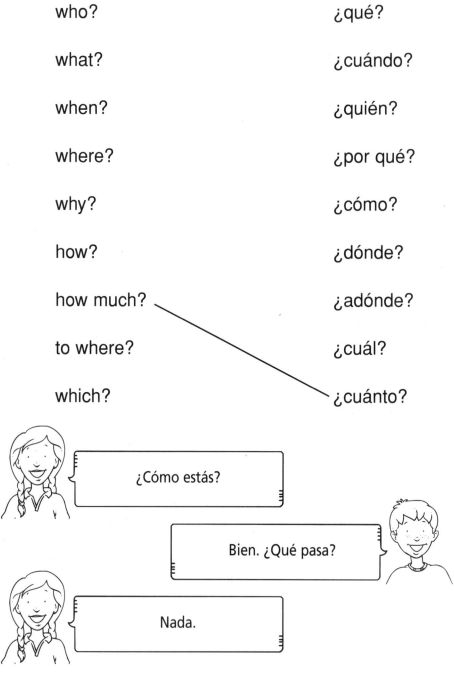

¿Cómo estás?

Bien. ¿Qué pasa?

Nada.

Vocabulario nuevo sobre la escuela—
New Vocabulary about School

Practice writing the school vocabulary words on the lines provided. Then say the words aloud.

1. lapiz (pencil) _____

2. pluma (pen) _____

3. papel (paper) _____

4. hoja (sheet of paper) _____

5. texto (textbook) _____

6. cuaderno (notebook) _____

7. escritorio (school desk) _____

8. sacapuntas (pencil sharpener) _____

9. borrador (eraser) _____

10. alumno/alumna (student) _____

11. maestro/maestra (teacher) _____

Vocabulario nuevo sobre la escuela—
New Vocabulary about School

1. matemáticas (math)_____

2. ciencias (science) _____

3. geografía (geography) _____

4. música (music)_____

5. arte (art) _____

6. educación física (physical education) _____

7. el recreo (recess) _____

8. historia (history) _____

9. inglés (English) _____

10. español (Spanish) _____

11. idioma (language) _____

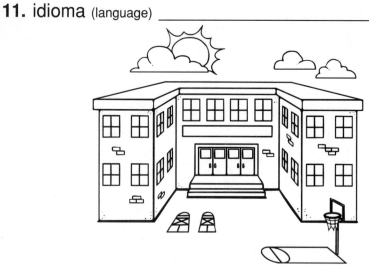

Acciones en la escuela—
Actions at School

Here are some Spanish verbs you might hear at school. Write the YO (I) form of each verb in the space as shown. Then practice saying the Spanish verb forms aloud.

	Leer (To read)		
(I)	Leo	Leemos	(we)
(you)	Lees		
(he, she, or it)	Lee	Leen	(they)

	Aprender (To learn)		
(I)		Aprendemos	(we)
(you)	Aprendes		
(he, she, or it)	Aprende	Aprenden	(they)

	Escribir (To write)		
(I)		Escribimos	(we)
(you)	Escribes		
(he, she, or it)	Escribe	Escriben	(they)

	Escuchar (To listen)		
(I)		Escuchamos	(we)
(you)	Escuchas		
(he, she, or it)	Escucha	Escuchan	(they)

	Trabajar (To work)		
(I)		Trabajamos	(we)
(you)	Trabajas		
(he, she, or it)	Trabaja	Trabajan	(they)

	Estudiar (To study)		
(I)		Estudiamos	(we)
(you)	Estudias		
(he, she, or it)	Estudia	Estudian	(they)

Frases escolares—School Phrases

Circle the correct form of each verb in the sentences. Remember that the verb must agree with the noun it modifies. If needed, refer to the previous page to verify which form is correct. Then say the sentence aloud.

1. La maestra dice que los alumnos ((trabajan) trabajo   trabajamos) por un hora todos los días.
(The teacher insists that the students **work** for an hour.)

2. Rosa (aprenden   aprendo   aprende) a dibujar muy bien en su clase de arte.
(Rosa **learns** how to draw very well in her art class.)

3. Si yo (estudian   estudio   estudias) matemáticas cada día, mis padres están contentos.
(If I **study** math every day, my parents are satisfied.)

4. Los estudiantes que (escuchamos   escucho escuchan) al maestro aprenden más.
(The students who **listen** to the teacher learn more.)

5. Nosotros (escriben   escribimos   escribes) mejor ahora, porque practicamos más.
(We **write** better now because we practice more.)

6. "Oye, Beto, ¿(leen   leo   lees) el nuevo libro sobre básquetbol?
(Listen, Beto, have you **read** the new book about basketball?)

Rompecabeza: palabras escolares—
School Words Crossword Puzzle

Complete the puzzle using Spanish words.

Down

1. eraser
3. pencil sharpener
4. sheet of paper
6. male teacher
7. pen
9. female student
12. textbook

Across

2. school desk
5. male student
7. paper
8. Spanish
10. pencil
11. female teacher
13. notebook

¿Cómo escribo la tarea sin lapiz?
(How do I write the homework without a pencil?)

Te presto el mío.
(I'll lend you mine.)

¡Búsca subjetos escolares!—
School Subjects Word Search

Word Bank

músíca
(music)

matemática
(math)

educación física
(physical education)

inglés
(English)

ciencia
(science)

el recreo
(recess)

idioma
(language)

geografía
(geography)

historia
(history)

arte
(art)

```
n a q p j h p w k u a b e h w p r b
h e k u h y k y b r n c n t e l b l
h e p j r g c n a z m a i e r x b x
s w q m k n v s e l g n i s k a j o
u l g o i d i o m a k a f n u u z y
h a i r o t s i h w v p x s s m t d
f s b y v r z o m a t e m a t i c a
b f k x e y i c b l f q l v i l a v
q t a i c n e i c d k s v x p r x u
l n d u k b y s e c m e c y e c n x
m v g p o y c e l r e c r e o q r b
e d u c a c i o n f i s i c i a l y
u t w a i f a r g o e g j a r e g t
```

"¡Tengo seis textos!"
(I have six textbooks!)

Repaso de frases interrogativas—
Review of Interrogative Phrases

Practice writing out the vocabulary words.

Word Bank

¿quién?
(who?)

¿qué?
(what?)

¿cuándo?
(when?)

¿dónde?
(where?)

¿por qué?
(why?)

¿cómo?
(how?)

alumno
(student)

cuaderno
(notebook)

tarea
(homework)

lapiz
(pencil)

ciencias
(science)

el recreo
(recess)

matemáticas
(math)

texto
(textbook)

geografía
(geography)

inglés
(English)

maestra
(teacher)

1. ¿_____ está tu _____ de _____?
(How is your math teacher?)

2. ¿_____ están mi _____ y mi _____?
(Where is my pencil and my notebook?)

3. ¿_____ es la _____ de _____ de hoy?
(What is the science homework for today?)

4. ¿_____ es tan pesado el _____ de _____ ?
(Why is the textbook for geography so heavy?)

5. ¿_____ es el nuevo _____ de la clase de _____?
(Who is the new student in English class?)

6. ¿_____ es __ _____
(When is recess?)

Poema escolar aplaudido—School Clapping Poem

Here is a clapping poem in Spanish. At recess time, children face each other and clap hands rhythmically while singing or saying the poem. ¡Es muy divertido!

Gusanitos

Nadie me quieren

Todos me odian

Mejor como gusanitos

Como la cabeza

Saco lo de adentro

(slurping sound)

¡MMM qué rico gusanito!

Little Worms

Nobody likes me

Everybody hates me

Guess I'll eat little worms.

Eat the head

Suck out the insides

(slurping sound)

MMM what delicious little worms!

La maestra no permite este poema durante la clase.
(The teacher doesn't allow this poem during class.)

Los cognados y las palabras similares—Cognates and Similar Words

The Spanish language was originally based on Latin, spoken by the Romans. The English language also contains many words with Latin roots. That's why so many Spanish words are already familiar to us. For example, **geografía** is obviously related to **geography**.

I've noticed that there are some Spanish words that aren't cognates but that have a clue. Like the word for *book*, **libro**. It has the same beginning as **library**.

And there are lots of books in libraries.

Write the English cognate for the Spanish vocabulary word in the space provided.

1. rápido

_____

6. tímido

_____

2. emoción

_____

7. historia

_____

3. poema

_____

8. arte

_____

4. matemáticas

_____

9. música

_____

5. ciencias

_____

10. computadora

_____

11. básquetbol

_____

12. practicar

_____

13. diferencia

_____

14. delicioso

_____

15. interesante

_____

16. precioso

_____

17. difícil

_____

18. importante

_____

19. inteligente

_____

20. nervioso

_____

Es muy interesante, ¿no?

¡Sí, y no es muy difícil!

Práctica con cognados y palabras similares—
Practice with Cognates and Similar Words

Write the correct Spanish word to complete each sentence, using cognates. Don't forget the accent marks.

1. George corre muy __rápido__ .
(George runs very fast.)

2. Los muchachos quieren _____ básquetbol después de estud'ar.
(The kids want to practice basketball after they study.)

3. A veces Rachel es un poco _____.
(Sometimes Rachell is a little timid.)

4. La mamá de Grayson hace un pastel _____.
(Grayson's mom makes a delicious cake.)

5. Mis ramos favoritos son _____ e _____.
(My favorite subjects are geography and history.)

6. El maestro de _____ es muy _____.
(The science teacher is very intelligent.)

Práctica con cognados y palabras similares—
Practice with Cognates and Similar Words

7. Grayson siempre usa su _____ para hacer su tarea.

(Grayson always uses his computer to do his homework.)

8. ¡El perrito nuevo es tan _____!

(The new puppy is so precious!)

9. Para Beto, _____ no es _____.

(For Beto, math is not difficult.)

10. La maestra dice que es _____ estudiar.

The teacher says that it's important to study.

11. Emilee saca buenas notas en _____.

(Emilee earns good grades in art.)

12. Rosa prefiere escribir un _____ cuando se siente creativa.

(Rosa prefers to write a poem when she feels creative.)

Vocabulario sobre los parientes—
Vocabulary about the Relatives

Practice writing the vocabulary words on the lines provided. Then say the words aloud.

1. madre   (mother)   _____

2. padre   (father)   _____

3. abuelo   (grandfather)   _____

4. abuela   (grandmother)   _____

5. tío   (uncle)   _____

6. tía   (aunt)   _____

7. primo   (male cousin)   _____

8. prima   (female cousin)   _____

9. sobrino   (nephew)   _____

10. sobrina   (niece)   _____

Vocabulario sobre los parientes—
Vocabulary about the Relatives

11. hermana (sister) _____

12. hermano (brother) _____

13. hijo (son) _____

14. hija (daughter) _____

15. bebé (baby) _____

16. suegra (mother-in-law) _____

17. suegro (father-in-law) _____

18. madrastra (stepmother) _____

19. padrastro (stepfather) _____

20. familia (family) _____

¡Hay muchos parientes en la reunión!
(There are lots of relatives at the reunion!)

Qué se les dice a los parientes—
What You Say to Relatives

Let's learn some phrases you might say when visiting with relatives. Complete each sentence with the correct vocabulary word. Then say the sentences aloud.

Word Bank

madre (mother)	tía (aunt)	hermana (sister)	suegra (mother-in-law)
padre (father)	primo (male cousin)	hermano (brother)	suegro (father-in-law)
abuelo (grandfather)	prima (female cousin)	hijo (son)	madrastra (stepmother)
abuela (grandmother)	sobrino (nephew)	hija (daughter)	padrastro (stepfather)
tío (uncle)	sobrina (niece)	bebé (baby)	familia (family)

---

1. _____, ¿le puedo traer a usted una taza de té?
(Grandma, can I bring you a cup of tea?)

2. Ah, niña, tienes la cara exactamente como la de tu
_____ y tu _____.
(Oh, child, you have a face exactly like your mother and your aunt.)

3. ¿Cuándo llega el _____ Tomás con nuestros _____?
(When does Uncle Tomas arrive with our cousins?)

4. Aquí hay un dólar para mi _____ favorito.
(Here's a dollar for my favorite nephew).

5. ¿_____ Tomás, hay un dólar para su _____ favorita
también?
(Uncle Tomas, is there a dollar for your favorite niece, too?)

Qué se les dice a los parientes—
What You Say to Relatives

6. ¿Juegas tú con tu _____ y tus _____ afuera?
(Do you play with your brother and your cousins outside?)

7. Nuestra _____ es muy grande.
(Our family is very big.)

8. Mi _____ tiene 86 años.
(Mi grandfather is 86 years old.)

9. Tengo dos _____ y una _____.
(I have two brothers and a sister.)

10. Grayson vive con su _____ y su _____.
(Grayson lives with his mother and his stepfather.)

Aparea a los parientes—
Match the Relatives Together

Draw a line between the corresponding vocabulary words as shown.

abuelo · · father

madre · · grandfather

padre · · mother

abuela · · uncle

tío · · grandmother

primo · · aunt

tía · · cousin (male)

sobrina · · cousin (female)

prima · · nephew

sobrino · · niece

Did you notice how the girl words end in *a* just like *always*?

Sí.

¡Busca los parientes!—
Relatives Word Search

Find and circle the Spanish vocabulary words.

Word Bank

hermana	hija	madrastra
hermano	bebé	padrastro
hijo	suegra	familia
	suegro	

```
b  q  m  t  u  h  e  r  m  a  n  o  f  w  k  h  u  w
a  b  z  j  b  a  t  w  w  c  d  j  n  i  y  h  i  z
z  r  z  h  m  v  j  a  r  t  s  a  r  d  a  m  z  x
o  p  h  p  c  a  b  w  o  s  j  k  d  h  d  u  c  a
l  e  e  l  a  w  r  j  z  s  h  k  q  b  j  q  k  l
g  t  r  f  t  z  t  f  w  u  a  h  b  y  p  o  m  h
f  v  m  v  y  w  e  x  h  q  i  e  b  e  b  j  w  c
a  m  a  a  r  g  e  u  s  j  l  u  b  w  y  i  i  a
u  a  n  n  w  d  b  o  a  h  i  f  q  i  t  h  p  l
u  y  a  q  a  z  o  r  x  y  m  w  f  w  m  c  b  v
a  d  o  r  g  e  u  s  r  g  a  q  l  p  y  j  d  k
k  v  f  j  s  f  m  b  j  p  f  f  w  h  r  c  n  p
o  r  t  s  a  r  d  a  p  p  u  b  u  a  y  q  e  u
```

¡Adiós!

Answer Pages

Page 5

Llegar
llego	llegamos
llegas	
llega	llegan

Pasar
paso	pasamos
pasas	
pasa	pasan

Bailar
bailo	bailamos
bailas	
baila	bailan

Comprar
compro	compramos
compras	
compra	compran

Gritar
grito	gritamos
gritas	
grita	gritan

Prestar
presto	prestamos
prestas	
presta	prestan

Page 6

Comer
como	comemos
comes	
come	comen

Escribir
escribo	escribimos
escribes	
escribe	escriben

Cubrir
cubro	cubrimos
cubres	
cubre	cubren

Depender
dependo	dependemos
dependes	
depende	dependen

Correr
corro	corremos
corres	
corre	corren

Subir
subo	subimos
subes	
sube	suben

Page 7

Hacer
hago	hacemos
haces	
hace	hacen

Decir
digo	decimos
dices	
dice	dicen

Venir
vengo	venimos
vienes	
viene	vienen

Page 8

Tener
tengo	tenemos
tienes	
tiene	tienen

Ir
voy	vamos
vas	
va	van

Estar
estoy	estamos
estás	
está	están

Ser
soy	somos
eres	
es	son

Answer Pages

Page 9
pasa, pasa, pasa, gusta, Tengo, Quieren, escucharlo

Page 10
pasa, Quieren, jugar, Vamos, es, escoger

Page 11

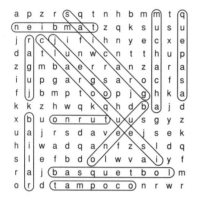

Page 12
1. bailar
2. escuchar
3. hablar
4. jugar
5. pasar
6. beber

Page 13

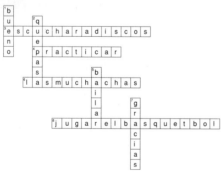

Page 15
1. la
2. unos
3. los
4. un

Page 17
1. niña, nueva, escuela, amigas, nuevas
2. Ella, sola
3. las, otras, muchachas, la, la, mesa, niñas
4. Ella, ellas, Elena

Page 18
1. un
2. una
3. Las   la   los
4. unos
5. un

Page 19
1. una
2. Un
3. una
4. Unas
5. un
6. unos

Page 20
1. los
2. La   el   la
3. Las   la
4. los
5. el
6. Los   la

Page 21
1. una
2. unos   una
3. un
4. un   un
5. un
6. unas

Page 22

grande	chico	rápido	lento
alto	bajo	feo	bonito
fuerte	débil	bueno	malo
gordo	flaco	antiguo	nuevo
mucho	poco	pobre	rico

Answer Pages

Page 24
1. grande
2. bonita   feos
3. nuevo   viejo
4. ricos   pobres   nuevo
5. fuerte   bueno
6. bueno

Page 26
1. tan grande como
2. no tan alto como
3. tan rápido como
4. no tan malo como
5. tan bonita como
6. tan chico como
7. tan grande como

Page 28
1. más deliciosa que
2. más precioso que
3. más divertido que
4. más difícil que
5. más interesante que
6. más divertido que
7. más feliz que

Page 30
1. la más importante
2. la más tranquila
3. los más inocentes
4. más delicioso
5. los más divertidos
6. los más inteligentes

Page 31

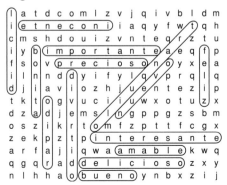

Page 32

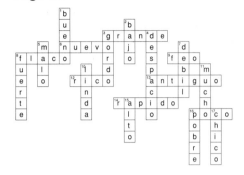

Page 35
1. algo
2. nada
3. también
4. siempre
5. nunca
6. tampoco
7. a veces

Page 36
8. algunos
9. también   ningún
10. o, o
11. De ningúna manera
12. ni, ni
13. de algún modo, alguien

Page 37

Answer Pages

Page 38

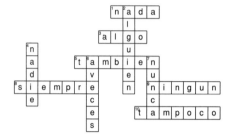

Page 39

pagar	comprar
vender	buscar
pedir ayuda	llevar
mirar	caro
barato	nuevo

Page 40

tienda	oferta
talla	precio
tarjeta de crédito	cheque
dinero	cambio
bolsa	vendedor(a)
ropa	zapatos
comida	vestidor

Page 41

1. llevar
2. pedir ayuda
3. buscar
4. mirar
5. pagar
6. vender
7. comprar

Page 42

1. tienda — oferta — ropa
2. dinero — precios
3. cheque — tarjeta de crédito
4. vendedora — zapatos — precio
5. vestidor
6. cambio — bolsa

Page 43

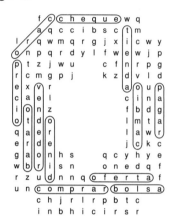

Page 44

1. zapatos
2. buscar
3. baratos
4. cambio
5. tienda
6. cheque
7. talla

Page 45

1. feliz
2. triste
3. cansado
4. tímido
5. tranquillo
6. amable
7. enojado
8. celoso
9. simpático
10. antipático
11. sorendido

Answer Pages

Page 46
12. deprimido
13. emocionado
14. contento
15. nervioso
16. enfermo
17. de buen humor
18. de mal humor
19. preocupado
20. desilusionado
21. aburrido
22. encantado

Page 47
1. sorpendida
2. alegres
3. contenta
4. nerviosa
5. preocupada
6. encantada

Page 48
7. deprimida
8. cansada   aburrida
9. de buen humor
10. tranquilo
11. feliz   feliz
12. celosa

Page 49

aburrido — surprised
sorpendido — nervous
enfermo — worried
nervioso — bored
preocupado — sick

contento — friendly
amable — calm
tranquilo — glad/satisfied
simpático — jealous
celoso — charming

tímido — happy
feliz — timid

Page 50

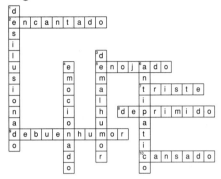

Page 51
¿quién?   ¿qué?
¿cuándo?   ¿dónde?
¿por qúe?   ¿cómo?

Page 52
¿cuánto?   ¿cuántos?
¿adónde?   ¿cuál?

Page 53
1. Quién
2. Cuándo
3. Cuándo
4. Dónde
5. Por qué
6. Cómo

Page 54

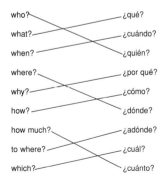

who? — ¿qué?
what? — ¿cuándo?
when? — ¿quién?
where? — ¿por qué?
why? — ¿cómo?
how? — ¿dónde?
how much? — ¿adónde?
to where? — ¿cuál?
which? — ¿cuánto?

Answer Pages

Page 55
1. lapiz
2. pluma
3. papel
4. hoja
5. texto
6. cuanderno
7. escritorio
8. sacapuntas
9. borrador
10. alumno/alumna
11. maestro/maestra

Page 56
1. matemáticas
2. ciencias
3. geografía
4. música
5. arte
6. educación física
7. el recreo
8. historia
9. inglés
10. español
11. idioma

Page 58
1. trabajan
2. aprende
3. estudio
4. escuchan
5. escribimos
6. lees

Page 59

Page 60

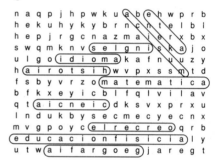

Page 61
1. Cómo   maestro/a   matemáticas
2. Dónde   lapiz   cuaderno
3. Cuál   tarea   ciencias
4. Por qúe   texto   geografía
5. Quién   estudiame   inglés?
6. Cuándo   el recreo

Page 63
1. rapid
2. emotion
3. poem
4. mathematics
5. science
6. timid
7. history
8. arte
9. music
10. computer

Answer Pages

Page 64
11. basketball
12. practice
13. different
14. delicious
15. interesting
16. precious
17. difficult
18. important
19. intelligent
20. nervous

Page 65
1. rápido
2. practicar
3. tímida
4. delicioso
5. geografía　　historia
6. ciencias　　inteligente

Page 66
7. computadora
8. precioso
9. matemáticas　　difícil
10. importante
11. arte
12. poema

Page 67
1. madre
2. padre
3. abuelo
4. abuela
5. tío
6. tía
7. primo
8. prima
9. sobrino
10. sobrina

Page 68
11. hermana
12. hermano
13. hijo
14. hija
15. bebé

16. suegra
17. suegro
18. madrastra
19. padrastro
20. familia

Page 69
1. Abuela
2. madre　　tía
3. tío　　primos
4. sobrino
5. Tío　　sobrina

Page 70
6. hermano　　primos
7. familia
8. abuelo
9. hermanos　　hermana
10. madre　　padrastro

Page 71

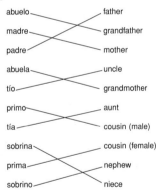

Page 72

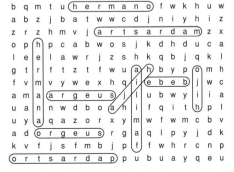

Notes

_____
_____
_____
_____
_____
_____
_____
_____
_____
_____
_____
_____
_____
_____
_____
_____
_____
_____
_____
_____

**Five things I'm
thankful for:**

1. _____
2. _____
3. _____
4. _____
5. _____